GOD'S

PROMISE

of

TODAY

Randy Petersen

Publications International, Ltd.

Randy Petersen is a writer and church educator from New Jersey with more than 40 books to his credit, including *All About Heaven, Praying Together,* and *Why Me, God?* A prolific creator of church curriculum, he's also a contributor to *Daily Dose of Knowledge: Bible* and *100 Fascinating Bible Facts.*

Cover photo: Goodshoot

ISBN-13: 978-1-4127-5287-9
ISBN-10: 1-4127-5287-6

Manufactured in China.

8 7 6 5 4 3 2 1

CONTENTS

Keeping His Word

※ ❈ ※

Great is thy faithfulness,
O God my Father…

You might recall singing the words above, celebrating the love of the Lord. As the music swells, it practically calls on us to trust him. We can always count on God. The Creator of the heavenly lights does not rise and set as they do. He gives us "every good gift and every perfect gift" with no "variableness" (James 1:17 KJV).

Hymns, Scriptures, countless sermons, and an increasing number of e-mail messages attest to the truth that our Lord keeps his promises. Believers can shout a healthy "amen" to that.

But what promises are we talking about? What exactly has he promised us? Has he promised to make us *happy* and *successful?* That depends what you mean by happy and successful. Still, joy and fulfillment are certainly among his many gifts.

Has he promised to remove all problems from our lives? Definitely not. He has actually assured us that following him brings on more problems.

Will he heal us of all our diseases? Yes, but not always in the way we want, and it may take a while—in fact, we might not find healing until we get to heaven.

Will he find a parking space for you, get you a raise, or make your noisy neighbors move out? Actually, he has been known to do things like that, but it's silly to get mad if he doesn't. The promises of God are far deeper, richer, and more life-changing.

Nowadays, there are books, seminars, and Web sites that basically offer you a blank check. *Whatever you want,* they say, *wish for it, focus on it, ask for it, claim it, or act as if you already have it—and you will attract it to yourself.* But any check is only as good as the bank from which it's drawn. While ambition, focus, and confidence can go a long way toward attaining your desires, God operates through relationships, not mind control. There's no magic wand here, no sacred incantation, no secret word that opens the heavenly storehouse. God wants to know you, to live with you, in you, and through you. In this world and the next, he vows to share his blessings with those who love him.

The Bible is full of God's promises. Some of these were made to specific people at specific times for specific reasons. Abraham and Sarah were promised children. David was promised a throne. Hezekiah was promised recovery from a terminal disease. But many other biblical promises extend rather obviously to the people of God, those who trust him to fulfill his promises. These commitments spring from his character and draw us deeper into a relationship with him.

For this book, we have chosen six promises. If we seek him, he will be found. He will love us forever. He forgives our sins. He showers us daily with new blessings. We will have trying times, but our temptations will never overwhelm us. He will strengthen us. There are surely other biblical promises that you can discover on your own, but these six seem basic to the kind of relationship God wants with us.

Great is his faithfulness, now and forever.

God wants to know you, to live with you,
in you, and through you. In this world and
the next, he vows to share his blessings
with those who love him.

CHAPTER 1
Seek and Find

When you search for me,
you will find me; if you seek me
with all your heart.

JEREMIAH 29:13

When you were a kid, did you ever play hide-and-seek too well? Maybe you found the perfect hiding place—inside an old trunk or under a pile of laundry. It was such a good spot that your playmates could never find you. They kept searching and calling—you heard their footsteps go right past you—but they could not discover your whereabouts.

It's a strange situation to be in, isn't it? In one sense, you have succeeded. You have won the game by finding the best hiding place. But your friends grow more and more frustrated as they search in vain. The game isn't fun anymore. In fact, they're talking about stopping and going somewhere else to play another game.

So what do you do? You cough, you move, or you do something to give yourself up. You're trying to make it fun again, to call the others back into the game. Maybe if you provide enough hints, they'll be able to find you after all.

Fast-forward a few years to another set of memories from your adolescence or perhaps from your 20s. Ah, young romance. You probably learned some lessons the hard way. For instance, when you throw yourself at someone, professing your undying love, they may run away. Also, if you're always there for someone, they may take you for granted. There is some wisdom in playing hard to get. If someone has to work to win your affection, they may treasure you more.

It's funny how the human heart works; it does play games with us. We tend to want what we can't have and undervalue what we do have. If we can "get" this partner easily, hey, maybe with some effort we can get an even better partner. Sure, it sounds crass to say it so bluntly, but that's how some people think. While there are relationships where mutual love blossoms from the start honestly and purely, this hard-to-get game is also common. Even if you haven't gone through it in your own life, you've surely seen it in the lives of others. And, as with hide-and-seek, some people can play hard to get too well. The person they're trying to attract might give up and go after someone a little easier to attain.

So, what do these youthful games have to do with the promises of God? Well, you might say that God sometimes plays hide-and-seek with us. And sometimes he plays hard to get. We all go through times in our lives when we feel distant from God, but this feeling does not need to be permanent. It's usually just God's way of helping us get to know him better or his way of wooing us into a deeper love for him. One major promise that gets repeated in various ways in Scripture is this: If we truly seek him, God will be found.

"For surely I know the plans I have for you," says the Lord, "plans for your welfare and not for harm, to give you a future with hope. Then when you call upon me and come and pray to me, I will hear you. When you search for me, you will find me; if you seek me with all your heart, I will let you find me," says the Lord.

JEREMIAH 29:11–14

BACK TO THE GARDEN

Let's go back to the beginning, to the Garden of Eden. You know the story of original sin, when Adam and Eve ate the forbidden fruit. But do you know what happened immediately afterward? God came looking for them, and they hid. "They heard the sound of the Lord God walking in the garden at the time of the evening breeze, and the man and his wife hid themselves from the presence of the Lord God among the trees of the garden. But the Lord

God called to the man, and said to him, 'Where are you?' He said, 'I heard the sound of you in the garden, and I was afraid, because I was naked; and I hid myself'" (Genesis 3:8–10).

Apparently, they were all in the habit of taking an evening stroll through this marvelous garden, but on that particular evening Adam and Eve hid from God. He even called to them to come out. Yes, this was the original game of hide-and-seek, but it was God doing the seeking.

Why were they hiding? They were ashamed. The serpent had said that partaking of the forbidden fruit would open their eyes to good and evil, making them like God. Like most of the tempter's deceptions, that was only half-true. It did open their eyes to good and evil, awakening within them a conscience they had never needed before, but it didn't make them the same as God. On the contrary, it showed them how different they were from God. How could they frolic with their Creator in the garden when they couldn't even follow his one and only rule? Becoming suddenly self-conscious, they grabbed fig leaves to cover the bodies God had made for them.

But it's still interesting that God called to them. He did not thunder his wrath or squash them like bugs. He was still angling for a relationship. Yes, their sin had changed everything. Yes, in a few minutes he'd utter the curse that would suddenly make life difficult. Yes, they would be banished from the garden, forced to leave paradise behind. They now had to live in a world of good and evil, joy and tears. The universe began its long groan for redemption. And yet God didn't disappear from human experience. Not at all. He provided an odd kind of parole for Cain, the first murderer, and he seemed to continue his daily walks with a man named Enoch. God kept seeking relationships with those who would come out of hiding.

This becomes the pattern throughout the early books of the Bible. God took the initiative, warning Noah about the flood, making a promise to Abraham, wrestling with Jacob, and dazzling Moses at the burning bush. Again and again, he sought to establish and develop a relationship with the people he had made. We might say that God has a crush on us.

TURNING AWAY FROM HIM

❄ ❄ ❄

Sadly, we also see another pattern in Scripture. When people are content with God's blessings, they forget about him. This was an ongoing cycle in the Old Testament. God established the Israelites in their own land, but they soon turned to corruption and idolatry, so he allowed foreign armies to oppress them. The Israelites then cried out to him for mercy, and he responded with victory and blessings, which they enjoyed until they forgot about him once more, and fell back into their bad habits. Round and round it went. But let's not be overly critical of the ancient Israelites. A similar cycle appears in the history of the Christian church and, if we're honest, we can see it in our own lives as well. When we know that God is crazy about us, we want to play the field.

Through the prophets, God often complained like a jilted lover: "'You have played the whore with many lovers; and would you return to me?' says the Lord" (Jeremiah 3:1). In fact, the Lord led one prophet, Hosea, to play out an object lesson about this in his own life. Hosea married a prostitute who wound up being unfaithful to him. This mirrored God's relationship with his people. Though he had provided for them, giving them security in their land and crops in season, they worshipped the local sky god, Baal, and thanked *him* for the rain. The Lord moans, "She has not acknowledged that I was the one who gave her the grain, the new wine and oil, who lavished on her the silver and gold—which they used for Baal" (Hosea 2:8 NIV).

Despite all his disappointment, the Lord kept begging for reconciliation. If they would return to him, he would forgive. "I will heal their disloyalty; I will love them freely" (Hosea 14:4). Through the prophet Isaiah, he says, "Come now, let us reason together. . . . Though your sins are like scarlet, they shall be as white as snow" (Isaiah 1:18 NIV). And, "Seek the Lord while he may be found, call upon him while he is near; let the wicked forsake their way, and the unrighteous their thoughts; let them return to the Lord, that he may have mercy on them, and to our God, for he will abundantly pardon" (Isaiah 55:6–7).

Even after their infidelity, God stood ready to forgive their sins, if only they would return to him. He wanted to bless them with the bounty of his love, but they had to want it first. "It is time to seek the Lord, that he may come and rain righteousness upon you" (Hosea 10:12).

Seek the Lord while he may be found, call upon him while he is near; let the wicked forsake their way, and the unrighteous their thoughts; let them return to the Lord, that he may have mercy on them, and to our God, for he will abundantly pardon.

ISAIAH 55:6–7

HARD TO GET

You can't blame God for trying a different strategy. If his constant appeals weren't working, maybe a cold shoulder would. What might happen if the Lord stepped back and let his people reap the consequences of their own misbehavior? Would they eventually realize that they needed him? Would they come running back and apologize for rejecting him?

"With their flocks and herds they shall go to seek the Lord, but they will not find him; he has withdrawn from them" (Hosea 5:6). What happened to "loving them freely"? Was God changing his policy? Apparently, yes. "I will return again to my place until they acknowledge their guilt and seek my face. In their distress they will beg my favour" (Hosea 5:15). God had played this game of hide-and-seek long enough. His people refused to come out of hiding and play with him, so he went home until they wised up.

Hosea's contemporary, Amos, was never one to mince words. "Seek the Lord and live," he said, "or he will break out against the house of Joseph like fire . . . with no one to quench it" (Amos 5:6). These are tough tactics: Seek him *or else!*

Historically, we see that this policy allowed the Israelites to be defeated by various enemies and even be carried away into captivity. In each case, there were some who learned their lesson. They sought the Lord once again and were welcomed back into his good graces. Jeremiah foresaw such a time: "In those days and at that time, says the Lord, the people of Israel shall come . . . weeping as they seek the Lord their God . . . they shall come and join themselves to the Lord by an everlasting covenant that will never be forgotten" (Jeremiah 50:4–5).

OUR JOURNEY

✻ ✻ ✻

If you're a stickler for precise theology, you might have had some problems with this chapter so far. Can we really speak of the actions of the mighty God in terms of a children's game or teenage romance? Granted, we lose something in the translation, but these examples might help us understand some of the patterns that pervade Scripture.

The truth is, we're not just talking about ancient Israel. This is our story, too. You have probably gone through times when God seemed far away. Maybe you're in a period like that now. You may remember how your heart used to burn with God's fire, how he seemed to be a part of every moment in your life. But now, not so much. Maybe you're still going through the motions of church involvement, or maybe you've let that slide, too.

This drifting away from God can happen for a number of reasons. Maybe it's **guilt.** Maybe, like Adam and Eve, you're sewing fig leaves together, ashamed of some deed that displeased God. You may cover yourself with religious activity, but you're not really taking those daily strolls with God anymore. Your heart is cold and afraid of intimacy.

Some people drift away because of **idolatry.** No, you're not bowing before "graven images" in your living room—unless that's what you'd call a big-screen, high-def TV. Come to think of it, a computer, a car, or even a house could be an idol. It could be your family, your favorite sport, or your political party. What is most important to you? What is taking God's place in your life? If you spend all your time and interest on something else, it's no wonder that God seems distant.

Others drift away because, well, they just **drift away.** Maybe your faith starts to get boring. You grabbed onto God a few decades ago to get through a rough patch, but things have been going pretty well lately—no need to overdo it. Prayers are pleasant. Bible reading is unremarkable. Church is okay, but it's usually about something other than God. Actually, marriages go through times like this, and it's fatal for some relationships. Partners stop wooing one another. They know each other so well, it's kind of boring. Tragically, this is when some marriages fall apart. The same sort of thing can happen in relationships with God.

There's one more reason for drifting away that we should discuss. You might call it **being spoiled.** Some of us can become like that precocious child who must have everything NOW. If God doesn't meet our needs instantly, we sulk. When things don't turn out well for us, despite all of our prayers, we get upset with God. Some folks hold grudges against God for years, and this can definitely dampen a relationship.

But that's where God might be playing hard to get. It's good for us to learn patience. If God gave us everything we wanted instantly, we'd treat him like a supernatural butler. It's better when we figure out that a relationship goes both ways. We do things for each other.

What's the solution? *Seek God!* Get in the game. Learn all you can about him. Do the things that he likes and avoid the things he doesn't. Tell him how much he means to you, and tell others, too. Listen to his ideas and share your innermost secrets. Come out of hiding and bring your authentic self before him. Let him amaze you.

God promises that when we seek him, he will be found. Even if there has been distance in the relationship in the past, that gap will close quickly once you take steps in his direction. The Lord made this promise to Solomon, no doubt foreseeing the upcoming ups and downs in his relationship with his people: "If my people who are called by my name humble themselves, pray, seek my face, and turn from their wicked ways, then I will hear from heaven, and will forgive their sin and heal their land" (2 Chronicles 7:14).

*God promises that when we seek him,
he will be found.*

That promise applied to their *land* and it applies to our *lives*. If God has seemed absent from your life, maybe it's because you haven't had room for him. If he feels far away, open your heart and move toward him. This game of hide-and-seek isn't child's play. God deeply wants to be found.

A Prayer from the Promise

Lord, I'm not sure what happened. I moved, or you moved, or both, but suddenly I'm acting as if you don't matter. You're a hazy memory from long ago and far away.

That's not what I want. I'm not sure how to fix this, but I'm tired of just going through the motions. I want you really, actively, in my life—today, tomorrow, and forever.

I know I've done some things to annoy you. Honestly, there are some things you've done that I'm not so crazy about. We're going to talk about those things. I know I don't even deserve to be in this conversation, but that's what you've promised, right? We're going to "reason together." You're going to forgive my sins (and there are plenty), and I'm going to surrender to you (which won't be easy).

I am making it my passion to seek you. Draw me nearer.

In your holy name, I pray. Amen.

CHAPTER 2
I Will Love You Forever

I have loved you with an everlasting love.

JEREMIAH 31:3

If you've bought an appliance lately, the salesperson probably tried to hawk an extended warranty for it. As if electronics stores don't already get enough of your money, they try to sell you some "security" based on an uncertain future. Perhaps you had the moxie to say, "So you're telling me that this product is so badly made, it will break down in year two?"

Of course, appliances sometimes do break down while you're still making payments on them or else they become obsolete. Your computer might still be humming along after three years, but it's now too slow, too big, or it doesn't have enough disk space for the new programs you want to run. We live in a temporary culture, and chances are you have a closet, basement, or garage crammed with formerly state-of-the-art items that are now classified as junk.

Good thing we don't treat *people* like that.

Er, um, maybe we do. Tonight on some talk show, a starlet will gush about her current beau, Frank—the love of her life. They have a "meaningful" relationship, beyond all the normal Hollywood nonsense, and they are "deeply committed" to each other in a "soul-to-soul connection." She might even show off a tattoo of his name— that proves it's for real.

Next year, that same starlet will appear again, explaining that she and her beau had "different goals," they weren't really in the "same place," and she came to this "painful realization" shortly after she started working with her new costar, a "brilliant" actor with whom she now has an even "more meaningful" relationship. And with the help of a skilled tattoo artist, the name FRANK easily became THANKS, which expresses her gratitude for the wonderful new man in her life.

〜

To think that love
could be everlasting simply
boggles the mind.

〜

We can make fun of the shallowness of the entertainment industry, but we all know similar situations from our own neighborhoods. Divorce is all too common.

Relationships that seemed to be built on undying love grow brittle and break. The long-term marriage of 50, 40, even 20 years is becoming the exception rather than the rule. Apparently, even true love doesn't always last.

That's why God's promise, delivered through Jeremiah, strikes us so powerfully. "I have loved you with an everlasting love," he says. In our society we don't know what *everlasting* means. We have to blink a few times and read the word again. To think that love could be everlasting simply boggles the mind.

JEREMIAH WAS A BULLDOG

We might assume that God was delivering this message to people he really liked, people who were faithful and obedient. If he pledged his eternal love to someone, they must have been doing something right. This had to be a high point in God's relationship with them. They were madly in love with him and he with them—right?

We could assume that, but we would be wrong.

Jeremiah spent most of his career warning of disaster. He was the ancient equivalent of the guy on the street corner with a megaphone yelling, "Repent! Now!" When people saw him coming, they walked the other way. His basic message was this: "You have offended God by tolerating idolatry, practicing corruption, and ignoring the poor. Therefore, God will punish this nation by bringing the Babylonians to conquer us."

That's not the kind of message people wanted to hear. Was Jeremiah a Babylonian sympathizer? He sounded like a traitor, as if he *wanted* the nation of Judah to fall. Besides, didn't he realize that the majestic Temple of Solomon was right there in Jerusalem? How could God ever let foreigners conquer and desecrate his own Temple? The nation's leaders ignored Jeremiah's warnings and continued their wicked ways.

———— ～ ————

I am with you and will save you . . .
I will discipline you but only with justice.
JEREMIAH 30:11 NIV

———— ～ ————

For this reason, Jeremiah is known as "The Weeping Prophet." He had an unpopular message that even he didn't want to deliver, yet he suffered arrest, threats, and confinement to do so.

Chapters 30–33 of the Book of Jeremiah are sometimes known as the Book of Hope. Tucked in the middle of dismal prophecies, this section talks about a brighter future. What happened *after* the Babylonians prevailed? God made it clear that he would restore the land after a time of judgment. He had big plans for his people.

"I am with you and will save you...," he said. "I will discipline you but only with justice" (30:11 NIV). "So you will be my people, and I will be your God" (30:22 NIV). "Again I will build you.... Again you shall take your tambourines, and go forth in the dance of the merrymakers" (31:4). "I will turn their mourning into joy, I will comfort them, and give them gladness for sorrow" (31:13). "There is hope for your future" (31:17).

This stunning burst of expectancy underscores a theme we find throughout the Bible: **God's love comes to those who don't deserve it.** Though these people had been ignoring and mistreating God's prophet, they still received this message of love. In fact, Jeremiah got arrested again *while he was composing these hopeful prophecies!*

I will turn their mourning into joy,
I will comfort them,
and give them gladness for sorrow.

JEREMIAH 31:13

"The word of the Lord came to Jeremiah a second time, while he was still confined in the court of the guard: ...'Call to me and I will answer you, and will tell you great and hidden things that you have not known.... I am going to bring... recovery and healing; I will heal them and reveal to them abundance of prosperity and security. . . . I will cleanse them from all the guilt of their sin against me, and I will forgive all the guilt of their sin and rebellion against me'"(33:1–8). We might expect God to say, "Let the prophet go, and then we'll talk about restoration," but he instead expressed his love for his people even while they sinned against him.

That's good news for us, because we share a trait with those ancient persecutors. We're sinful too. In case you thought that you were somehow excluded from God's declaration of everlasting love because you just don't measure up, think again. His love is based on who he is, not who we are.

The New Testament confirms this aspect of divine love. "God proves his love for us in that while we still were sinners Christ died for us"(Romans 5:8). Though we share in the sin of Jeremiah's tormentors, we also share in the everlasting love of God.

THE TRANSFORMER

Jeremiah's prophecies of hope also touch on another aspect of this divine love: **It changes us.** "I will put my law within them, and I will write it on their hearts," said the Lord (Jeremiah 31:33). The people had been encountering God's truth as something outside of them, something they could choose to engage or not. That's the way it is with many people today, even some religious folks. They have respect for the word of God, but it's something on a shelf somewhere or stored away in a trunk. They can pull it out in a pinch, but why bother? Yet, the transforming love of God gets inside us. He inscribes his truth on our minds and bathes our hearts in his word. We learn to care about what he cares about.

Again, the New Testament picks up this theme. Jesus promised that the Holy Spirit would "guide you into all the truth"(John 16:13), and other passages refer to the Spirit being in our hearts, transforming our attitude and behavior. It's an inside job. The knowledge of what God wants isn't on a shelf somewhere—it's within us, challenging and changing us.

One of the classic stories of Christian ministry in modern times is *The Cross and the Switchblade* by David Wilkerson. He was a preacher from rural Pennsylvania who felt a call from God to go to New York City and share the gospel with kids in street gangs. Even he thought it was crazy, but like Jeremiah he obeyed the call. Bold and naive, he walked into a violent world with a simple message: "God loves you." He was laughed at. He was threatened. But many of the hardened gang members needed to hear exactly what he had to say. Love had been squeezed out of their environment, but now this preacher was in their face about it, challenging them to think about it, to feel it, to see themselves as people loved by their Creator. And it seems that the message gained power because the messenger himself was demonstrating love toward them. Wilkerson was being transformed by God's love into an adventurous evangelist—scared silly but absolutely driven.

The knowledge of what God wants isn't on a shelf somewhere—it's within us, challenging and changing us.

When one young tough named Nicky Cruz threatened to stab him, Wilkerson replied, "You could cut me in a thousand pieces and lay them out in the street, and every piece would love you." In time, Cruz was transformed by this divine love. He came to faith and eventually became an evangelist himself.

Look around you. How many people do you pass each day who need to hear this promise? How many people are looking for love, lacking love, or losing love for themselves? Your friends and neighbors long to hear this note of hope: "I have loved you with an everlasting love."

Think of how it could transform their lives. Think of how it could transform *you*.

This promise is not something to be nodded at. It requires more than an "Okay, fine." Don't analyze it or explain it away. Don't write a blog entry on it. It's more than a cerebral experience.

How many people are looking
for love, lacking love,
or losing love for themselves?

Open yourself to it. Embrace it. Splash around in it. Splash some other people too. You are loved by God! Forever!

GRASP IT

In the middle of his letter to the Ephesians, the Apostle Paul launched into a prayer for them: "And I pray that you, being rooted and established in love, may have power, together with all the saints, to grasp how wide and long and high and deep is the love of Christ, and to know this love that surpasses knowledge—that you may be filled to the measure of all the fullness of God"(Ephesians 3:17–19 NIV).

In a way, this is a prayer for us, too. "All the saints" refers not just to special, canonized individuals but rather to all believers, including us. So what does Paul want for us?

He wants us to be "rooted and established" in love. *Rooted* suggests not only stability but also nourishment. A plant draws sustenance through its roots, just as we are nourished through God's love. The love of God gives us the strength to live each day. It feeds our growth. *Established* is more of a building term: God's love is our foundation. Everything else we do rests on that certainty.

He wants us to grasp the magnitude of divine love. *Grasp* is a great word there, because it's not just mental. It can refer to physically grabbing something, literally embracing it. The thought is not only that we understand the vastness of Christ's love for us, but also that we experience every part of it.

———

A plant draws sustenance through its roots, just as we are nourished through God's love. The love of God gives us the strength to live each day.

———

He wants us to know this love, even though it surpasses knowledge. There's some wordplay here, on several levels. "Knowing the unknowable" is the goal, but again that suggests the knowledge is not just about facts. Knowing people involves more than a checklist of details about their lives. It means you're in some sort of relationship with them. So, Paul prays that we would enter into a relationship with the love of God, which calls us into ever-increasing intimacy.

It's also possible that Paul was taking a shot at a cult group that was beginning to form in the church, the Gnostics. (Several books in the last few years have been promoting Gnostic teaching, but the New Testament writers opposed it.) Gnostics tended to teach that a secret knowledge *(gnosis)* allowed some lucky people into a special relationship with God. Jesus was for beginners, they said. As you advanced, you could get to know higher angelic beings. In that light, Paul might have been claiming that the love of Christ surpasses the *gnosis* of the Gnostics. We must go far beyond any secret knowledge, he says, and experience the vast ocean of Christ's unfathomable love.

SKY TO SKY

There's a hymn called "The Love of God" that people love to sing—especially the majestic third verse. A minister named Frederick M. Lehman, who, at the time, was working at a fruit-packing company, composed it. Inspired by a sermon he had heard about God's love, he started writing a stanza one morning at breakfast.

The love of God is greater far
Than tongue or pen can ever tell;
It goes beyond the highest star,
And reaches to the lowest hell;

He had to go to work and lift crates of oranges and lemons, but he resumed the composition at break time. Soon he had two verses and this chorus.

O love of God, how rich and pure!
How measureless and strong!
It shall forevermore endure
The saints' and angels' song.

Later at home, Lehman pounded out a melody on an old upright piano. He still felt he needed a third verse, but nothing was coming. Then he remembered a poem he had heard at a religious camp meeting. It was printed on a card, but where had he put it? He then remembered that he was using it as a bookmark. The words fit his melody perfectly—until he noticed the fine print: "These lines were found in translated form on the walls of a patient's room in an insane asylum after the patient's death." That freaked him out a little, but then he noticed that the lines were translated from the Aramaic language and were originally written by a Jewish cantor named Meir Ben Isaac Nehorai, in Worms, Germany, in the year 1050.

So the following eight lines, echoing the sentiments of Paul's prayer, came from a German synagogue, through an insane asylum and then a fruit-packing company, to the hearts of millions of worshipers.

> *Could we with ink the ocean fill,*
> *And were the skies of parchment made,*
> *Were every stalk on earth a quill,*
> *And every man a scribe by trade,*
> *To write the love of God above,*
> *Would drain the ocean dry.*
> *Nor could the scroll contain the whole,*
> *Though stretched from sky to sky.*

A Prayer from the Promise

I can't begin to understand the magnitude
of your love for me, Lord, but I thank you for
it. It astonishes me that you can love someone
like me, a messed-up sinner.
Oh, I try to pretend that I've got everything
under control, but you and I both know
that I don't deserve one ounce of your love.
And yet you say you love me, eternally.

So bring it on! Love me as much as you can.
I am going to open my heart as wide as it can
go, and you may need to pry it even wider.
Let your love fill me.
Let it transform me. Let it overflow to others.
Let everyone come to know me
as One Who is Loved by God.

And all that's left to say is thank you.
And, I love you too.
Amen.

CHAPTER 3
I Will Forgive Your Sins

I will forgive their iniquity,
and remember their sin no more.

JEREMIAH 31:34

It was a story that shocked and saddened the nation. One Monday morning a crazed gunman entered a school in Nickel Mines, Pennsylvania, and shot 10 girls, ages 6 to 13, killing 5. Then he shot himself.

The media flocked to the area, a tight-knit Amish community in Lancaster County, prepared to deliver another account of senseless violence. First Columbine, and now Nickel Mines. Where would it end? But reporters found quite a different story when they got there. Yes, the nation grieved as they saw footage of the mourning families attending one funeral after another. There were reconstructions of the crime, interviews with police detectives, and endless musings about who the murderer was and why he did it. But the headline from this largely faith-based community wasn't tragedy—it was forgiveness.

In interviews, one relative after another said they forgave the shooter: "If you have Jesus in your heart and he has forgiven you . . . [how] can you not forgive other people?" asked one woman, a midwife who helped deliver two of the slain girls. The grandfather of two victims was asked if he had forgiven the gunman. "In my heart, yes," he replied, "through God's help."

This didn't look like denial. These people didn't seem brainwashed. They weren't shrugging off this tragedy; rather, they were moving through it. Their grief was real, but so was their faith.

Perhaps the most dramatic act of forgiveness came when the community reached out to the widow of the murderer. In interviews, many stopped talking about their own pain to say that they were praying for the killer's family to have peace in this horrible time. Some even visited the widow to express their condolences. Others indicated she would be welcome at the victims' funerals.

Their grief was real, but so was their faith.

You wouldn't blame the people of Nickel Mines if they had lashed out in anger. Their children had their whole lives ahead of them. It wasn't right for them to be taken in this way. Why didn't people stop this killer? Why didn't they recognize the warning signs? Where did he get a gun? Why weren't there better security measures at the school? We would expect the families of the victims to be outraged, full of venom against the murderer, against society, against God. But that wasn't the story that came out of the grieving town. This was a mature community, rooted in their faith, and they understood the power of forgiveness.

IN THE BEGINNING, GOD

What is this power? Where does it come from? How does it get into our lives?

The power of forgiveness starts with God. As the midwife in Nickel Mines indicated, if we have received divine forgiveness, we have a compulsion to forgive others. How can we not? The opposite point seems true as well—the inability to forgive others may stem from a difficulty in receiving God's forgiveness.

In fact, reports from Nickel Mines indicate that the shooter was tormented by guilt. He reportedly left notes and a phone message referring to a secret crime from his past: In his youth, he had molested two girls in his family. We can only imagine how that guilt must have plagued his mind for 20 years. Did this memory drive him mad? It would be irresponsible for us to play amateur psychologist here, so we won't delve too deeply. It just seems that this man needed a way to set things right. He needed to face up to his youthful sin and bring it before God. Like so many in our world today, he desperately needed to hear the promise of God: "I will forgive your sins."

You might have an image of God as a stern judge, thundering from heaven to rule against human wickedness. Lots of people think of him that way, and as a result, they stay far away. They might engage in religious practices out of fear, but there's not much love involved. To be honest, that picture of God does exist in Scripture, but it's not the only one. In fact, it's not even the prevalent one. Just as you have different facets of your personality, so too does God. You might act sternly toward your children when they need to learn obedience, and you might even be angry with them on occasion. That doesn't mean you're an ogre.

So, yes, God is holy. He's also jealous; he hates it when we worship other gods. He gets angry at human wickedness, especially when the poor are exploited for the sake of pride or greed. But there's another side to our Creator that's expressed in the Old and New Testaments alike: *He understands our failings and is eager to forgive us.*

Nehemiah prayed, "You are a God ready to forgive, gracious and merciful, slow to anger and abounding in steadfast love" (Nehemiah 9:17). "When deeds of iniquity overwhelm us," the psalmist says, "you forgive our transgressions" (Psalm 65:3).

You are a God ready to forgive,
gracious and merciful, slow
to anger and abounding in steadfast love.

NEHEMIAH 9:17

If you are worried that you have sinned too much and don't deserve God's forgiveness, you're right—but you don't understand forgiveness. No one deserves it. Your sin doesn't disqualify you. In fact, you might say that sin is the main requirement for being forgiven. That was the Pharisees' problem: They wouldn't admit their sins, so they wouldn't ask for forgiveness (John 9:41). If you feel bad about sinning too much, God has you right where he wants you. Let the forgiving commence!

CLAY JARS

Skip was asked by his pastor to serve on a planning team for a church mission project. He said no.

"I don't want to twist your arm," the pastor pressed, "but you have the gifts, the passion, the ability. What's the problem?"

Skip looked down at the floor. "It's just that I've done some things I'm not proud of."

"Join the club!" the pastor laughed.

"No, really. I just don't think God can use me with what I've done."

The pastor let the matter slide for the moment but made a point to talk more with Skip in the future, and maybe to focus on the issue of forgiveness.

The truth is, if God only worked with sinless people, he wouldn't get much done. Look at our great biblical examples. Noah? On one occasion he got drunk and naked in public. Abraham and Sarah were models of faith, but Abraham tried to save his own skin once by putting Sarah in Pharaoh's harem. Rebekah played a nasty trick on her blind husband. Jacob was a notorious cheater. Judah slept with his daughter-in-law Tamar. Moses killed a guy. Aaron built a golden idol. Saul threw a spear at his harpist. Solomon had at least 900 more wives than he needed. Elijah got suicidal. James and John tried to call fire from heaven to devour those who disagreed with them. Peter denied knowing Jesus.

The truth is,
if God only worked with sinless people,
he wouldn't get much done.

Feet of clay? These heroes had *souls* of clay, but God forgave their sins and used them for his glory. The apostle Paul talked freely about his preconversion days as a persecutor of Christians: "Even though I was formerly a blasphemer, a persecutor, and a man of violence...the grace of our Lord overflowed for me with the faith and love that are in Christ Jesus. The saying is sure and worthy of full acceptance, that Christ Jesus came into the world to save sinners—of whom I am the foremost. But for that very reason I received mercy" (1 Timothy 1:13–16).

King David stands as a great figure in biblical history, a Renaissance man long before the Renaissance. Musician, poet, warrior, and ruler—he is called "a man after his [God's] own heart" (1 Samuel 13:14). And yet even he was guilty of a grievous sin. While the army was off at war, David committed adultery with the wife of one of his best soldiers. Then he tried to cover it up by engineering the death of this soldier in battle. Illicit sex led to murder, and David almost got away with it—until God sent the prophet Nathan to challenge him.

Faced with his sin, David repented publicly, wearing sackcloth and covering himself with ashes. His deeply personal psalm of confession made it into Israel's hymnbook. "Have mercy on me, O God," he wrote, "according to your steadfast love; according to your abundant mercy blot out my transgressions. Wash me thoroughly from my iniquity, and cleanse me from my sin....Create in me a clean heart, O God, and put a new and right spirit within me" (Psalm 51:1–2, 10).

The lesson? Past sin doesn't exclude you from God's plans. The experience of forgiveness may actually empower you to serve even more effectively. Paul, the former persecutor, talked about believers being dirty, fragile vessels for God's valuable message. "We have this treasure in clay jars, so that it may be made clear that this extraordinary power belongs to God and does not come from us" (2 Corinthians 4:7).

THE MECHANICS OF FORGIVENESS

How do we appropriate God's forgiveness? If it is available to us, how do we snag it?

First, we **confess** our sin. "If we confess our sins," the apostle John assures us, "he who is faithful and just will forgive us our sins and cleanse us from all unrighteousness" (1 John 1:9). But it's important to understand what confession is and isn't. It's not an excuse. It's not an explanation. It's not a defense before the court. It does not seek to minimize the offense. It's a recognition that we have done wrong and that we're sorry.

Our common language betrays us here. If you tell someone, "I'm sorry," you're likely to hear, "That's okay" or "No problem" or, in Spanish, "*De nada,* it's nothing."

And that exchange might be perfectly fine if you just bumped into someone as you walked down the street. But when we have sinned, it's *not* okay, it *is* a problem, and it's *something* we need to deal with. When you bring your sin before God, don't try to wriggle out of the responsibility. Confession means owning up to your mistake.

We could say that the first step, confession, is the only step necessary. After all, God's forgiveness comes out of his grace. It's a gift; we can't earn it. And yet Scripture mentions several other related actions. We might also show **signs of repentance.** John the Baptist challenged the Pharisees to "bear fruit worthy of repentance" (Matthew 3:8). They were gawkers, traveling down to the river to check out his baptizing show. John asked them to do something that showed they were serious about changing their lives.

In some churches, priests give people who confess some act of penance to perform, though some misinterpret the significance behind this. The idea is not to try to earn God's forgiveness through action, but to show that you're serious about turning away from your sin. Really, it's not a bad idea for you to find some action that signals your change of heart to God.

"Therefore **confess your sins to one another,**" James tells us, "and pray for one another, so that you may be healed" (James 5:16). This might be difficult, but it truly helps to have another believer praying for your spiritual healing and also holding you accountable.

Make things right. Jesus said that if your act of worship is interrupted by the thought that you have wronged someone, you should take a time-out and reconcile with that person before you come back to worship (Matthew 5:23–24). As much as possible, clear things up with anyone you've hurt. Make restitution where necessary.

When you bring your sin before God, don't try and wriggle out of the responsibility. Confession means owning up to your mistake.

In the days and weeks after your sin and forgiveness, take steps to grow. Of course, you may continue to be tempted in the same way, but you can use your God-given wisdom to live differently, establishing new patterns that steer clear of danger zones. When Jesus stopped people from stoning an adulterous woman, he didn't condemn her but challenged her to "leave your life of sin" (John 8:11 NIV).

Peter probably thought he was being very magnanimous when he asked Jesus if he should forgive someone seven times. Jesus surprised him by saying, "Not seven times, but, I tell you, seventy-seven times" (Matthew 18:22). The point is that **forgiveness often needs to be**

repeated, and we should be ready to offer it as often as necessary—and to ask for it. We do the same dumb things over and over. How often do we come before the Lord to say, "I'm sorry, again, please forgive me." The repeated cycles of biblical history confirm that God is ready to forgive us again and again and again and again.

"Forgive us our trespasses [or debts]," we pray, "as we forgive those who have trespassed against us [our debtors]." It's interesting that in Jesus' prototypical prayer, our forgiveness from God is linked to our forgiveness for others. This isn't some hoop for us to jump through in order to earn God's pardon, but it expresses a simple truth about forgiveness: **Forgiven people forgive others.** When you really *get* forgiveness, when you see that God has given you a blessing at the very moment you least deserve it, your heart breaks open and blessings spill out to those around you. As the woman in Nickel Mines said, "If you have Jesus in your heart and he has forgiven you... [how] can you not forgive other people?"

SIMPLY AMAZING

John Newton was a young man in the 1700s who became embroiled in the slave trade. As a boy, he worked aboard a merchant ship captained by his father, and he was drafted into the British navy but then went AWOL. Soon, he was bouncing around the ports of Africa, managing slave warehouses, and working on slave ships—eventually becoming captain of a slave ship.

One day, a fierce storm threatened to sink his ship. Though he was the least religious person imaginable, Newton cried out to God for help. Fearing death in the storm, he worried that he was too sinful to be saved. This event proved to be his conversion moment. Afterward, he wrote about the day of that storm as a time when "the Lord came from on high and delivered me out of deep waters." He continued seafaring for a while, studying the Bible whenever he could. Eventually, he returned to England, entered the ministry, and attained some fame as an earnest preacher and creative songwriter. Haunted by memories of his own complicity in the slave trade, he supported the growing abolition movement in England, led by William Wilberforce.

A movie about Wilberforce, called *Amazing Grace,* features Albert Finney in a strong cameo role as the elderly John Newton. In the first of two unforgettable scenes, he speaks of the 20,000 ghosts—the slaves he transported—that "live with me in this little church. There is still blood on my hands." We see a man tormented by sins of the past, humbly trying to make up for the wrongs he committed.

The second scene shows Newton beginning to dictate the story of his past in the slave trade, including grisly details. (As a point of historical fact, Newton did publish a pamphlet that raised awareness throughout England about the atrocities of slavery.) Though he had gone blind, there is a bounce in his step and a smile behind his eyes. Finney presents the image of a man who has embraced his own forgiveness. Relaying words that Newton actually said, Finney tells us: "Although my memory is fading, I remember two things very clearly: I'm a great sinner, and Christ is a great Savior."

God's promise of forgiveness is powerfully captured in the first verse of John Newton's most famous hymn:

> Amazing grace, how sweet the sound
> That saved a wretch like me
> I once was lost, but now am found
> Was blind, but now I see

A Prayer from the Promise

*Lord, you know exactly what I've done and what
I haven't done. You know my secret sins and my proud
mistakes. You know all about those moments when
I knew what was right and what was wrong, and I chose
the wrong. You know about my rebellion, my lust, and
my selfishness. You know how often I try to live as if
I don't need you. And there's probably something else
I'm forgetting, but you know that too.
I come before you as a sinner.*

I am sorry.

*That sounds kind of weak, but it's true. I am sorry for
hurting you, for disobeying you, for thinking I knew
better than you did. I'm sorry. And I want to do better.
I want to make things right. My life needs to change.*

*But for right now I'm grabbing your promise.
You're telling me you will forgive my iniquity and forget
my sin. I'm counting on that promise; I'm trusting it.
Create in me a clean heart—through your kindness,
your grace, and your sacrifice.*

Thank you, Lord. Amen.

CHAPTER 4

I Give You Daily Blessings

❧ ❧ ❧

His mercies...are new every morning.

LAMENTATIONS 3:22–23

The acting class begins with a warm-up. In a few minutes they'll limber up their backs, arms, and legs, but they begin by stretching their minds, specifically their *senses*.

"Stand in a straight, relaxed posture and breathe," the teacher says. "What do you hear right now?" There's silence for a few seconds, then the hum of the heating system, a car outside with a bad muffler, and the growl of someone's stomach. Some of these teenagers haven't experienced this kind of quiet all day.

"What do you feel?" the teacher goes on. "The air on your arms and face? The weight of your body on your feet? Now take a deep breath. What do you smell?"

Then comes the best part. "Close your eyes and spin slowly in your own space. Just rotate, then stop and open your eyes. What do you see? Is there something in this room that you've never paid attention to before? See it. Register it. Now close your eyes and rotate again. Stop, open your eyes, and see something else you've never noticed before." They do this a third time and then pause to talk about what they have seen.

"That mark on the exit sign."

"There's a little dent in the wall over there."

"The corner of that poster."

"The map of Europe on the wall."

Some of the students have been in this room hundreds of times. They have seen these things again and again, but they hadn't really noticed them until today. The teacher hopes that they will leave the room and pay more attention to the world around them. Acting requires strong observational skills, as does any art form. You might say the same thing about the art of abundant living.

"The steadfast love of the Lord never ceases," affirmed the prophet Jeremiah, "his mercies never come to an end; they are new every morning; Great is your faithfulness" (Lamentations 3:22–23). The Lord keeps coming at us with new "mercies." The blessings of his love surprise us each day, if only we open our eyes to them. The hymn based on this verse puts it beautifully: *Morning by morning new mercies I see.* But do we really see these expressions of God's love? Too often we walk right past them.

We're busy people. We fill our schedules with both work and play. Nowadays preteens carry computerized appointment books, and retirees have more responsibilities than they had when they were working. Ask a friend, "How are you?" and your friend will probably say, "Busy." We've become masters of multitasking. If we have a minute to kill, we're on our cell phones. We're so concerned about getting from Point A to Point Z that we completely miss Points B through Y. Every morning we walk right past the new mercies that God has given us, because we're too distracted to notice them.

Even when we do slow down, we can still miss these mercies because we're so focused on ourselves. Not that we're proud or conceited—we just pay more attention to our own needs and concerns than anything else God brings into our world. Even overly humble people can be very self-focused if they always worry about their own failings. If God wants to speak a word of encouragement into your life, don't contradict it!

Then, there are some people who have just turned sour, which causes them to overlook the blessings of God. Maybe they have good reasons for this, such as painful experiences they can't quite forget. Still, they're quick to complain and slow to rejoice. They see a world going downhill fast, and they think they're being devout by calling attention to every godless thing they see, but in the process they turn a blind eye to the redemptive acts of God happening all around them.

And some folks just get so used to doing things a certain way and think there's no room for surprise. They think they know what's around them, so they stop looking. They have a deep faith in God, and they rest in the assurance that he will never change. They think they already know the way God works, so they stop expecting new mercies.

We all need to stop, relax, and breathe the fresh air of the Holy Spirit. Like the acting students, we need to turn ourselves around to a new position, open our eyes, and see things from a new angle. We need to pay attention to things that may have always been there but only now sparkle with the fingerprints of the Creator. We need to use all of our senses, physical and spiritual, to drink in the new mercies that God gives us every morning.

So take a barefoot walk in the grass and feel the miracle of photosynthesis. Exult in the beauty of a crisp blue sky or the drama of an approaching storm. Or marvel at the extent of human endeavor—the God-given ability to plan, organize, and construct a skyscraper, for instance. It may be that someone will hold a door open for you today at a store or your workplace, or maybe someone will pause at the door to make sure it doesn't slam in your face. Those are everyday kindnesses you can appreciate.

Sure, we live in a dog-eat-dog world with depraved humans fending for themselves, but there are still some drivers who let you into a lane of traffic or shopkeepers who say, "Have a nice day," and mean it.

Try it sometime: Go out for a stroll or a drive and start counting the kindnesses of God. You'll be amazed at what you start to see.

DEEPEST FEELINGS

Jeremiah used two interesting words for the "steadfast love" of God and his mercies. The first is the Hebrew word *hesed.* This word is pretty common in the Old Testament, especially in the Book of Psalms. Some translations read it as "loving kindness" or "compassion." Sometimes regular people show *hesed,* but usually God is the one giving it out. So once again we're promised the love of God but not in a nebulous theological sense. The word *hesed* refers to the specific expressions of God's love—the many kind things he does for people.

Scholars make another fascinating observation about this word—it originated in the language of contracts and agreements. A worker with *hesed* could be counted on to fulfill a contract *and then some.* When applied to God, it means he keeps his promises but also throws in some extras. He does everything we expect of him and more.

*Our God has incredibly deep feelings for us,
and he shows us his love every day of our lives.*

The second word, *rechem,* is parallel to *hesed* and similar in meaning, but it brings us to a whole new level—to the new mercies we receive each morning. In many translations, the word literally means "womb." You might call it "motherly love"—both the deep-seated compassion that a mother feels for her children and the many practical things she does for them as a result. The word *rechem* describes perhaps the strongest bond we know as humans. It is not surprising that in the Old Testament, the word is often used to portray God's love for us.

Our God has incredibly deep feelings for us, and he shows us his love every day of our lives.

RESPONDING TO GOD'S MERCIES

How should we respond to God's awesome love? Well, we've already discussed our first response, which is simply to see it in action. But we should add another challenge. Sometimes God's mercies don't look like mercies. They may not look like good things at all. Still, we may be forced into unpleasant circumstances that turn out to be gifts from God. It would be natural to complain about the inconvenience, the disappointment, or the pain of these moments, but is it also possible to see them as more of God's daily mercies?

"Whenever you face trials of any kind," James tells us, "consider it nothing but joy, because you know that the testing of your faith produces endurance" (James 1:2–3). He's talking about a way of seeing things, by turning ourselves around and viewing our trials from a different angle.

Paul wrote to the Philippians from prison, and yet the epistle is full of joy. "I want you to know, beloved," he said of his imprisonment, "that what has happened to me has actually helped to spread the gospel" (Philippians 1:12). He saw his difficulties in a positive light.

G. K. Chesterton, a brilliant Christian author from a century ago, quipped, "An inconvenience is just an adventure wrongly considered." The trick for us is to change the way we consider things. How would it alter your attitude if you looked at every inconvenience as an opportunity, given by God, to begin a character-building adventure?

A second response is to **give thanks.** This follows logically: If we go through life recognizing every moment—both pleasant and unpleasant—as a gift from God, we will naturally want to thank him for everything. "Give thanks in all circumstances," writes Paul (1 Thessalonians 5:18).

Let's think about giving thanks. Where does an attitude of gratitude come from? Is it the sort of feeling we can rev up whenever we want, or does it depend on what's happening to us at the moment? Paul added "And be thankful" to a collection of exhortations (Colossians 3:15), as if he were only adding milk or bread to a shopping list. Is it really that easy? Can we just decide to *be* thankful?

Perhaps we can get into this question from the opposite side. What about people who are *unthankful?* What's the problem with them? A guy drops his wallet on the street and you run after him to return it. He takes it back without a word or even a grunt of appreciation. Does he think he is *entitled* to your good deed? Does he think the universe owes him a favor and you're just giving him back what he deserves? Or does he suspect you filched the wallet to begin with?

Expectations play a huge role in gratitude. British writer C. S. Lewis uses the example of a hotel stay to illustrate this point. Imagine two people staying in the same hotel, a place of average quality. One was told it was a dive while the other expects four-star luxury. The first person will then be delighted the place is as good as it is, while the second will complain about everything. The lesson? If you go through life with a sense of entitlement, giving thanks will be difficult. You will tend to see the kindnesses of God and others as *givens.* But how would it change your attitude if you expected nothing? Would you suddenly allow yourself to be surprised by the great, unexpected blessings that come your way?

The Book of Psalms, of course, is full of praise and thanks offered to the Lord. "Enter his gates with thanksgiving, and his courts with praise," says one majestic psalm. "Give thanks to him, bless his name. For the Lord is good; his steadfast love endures for ever, and his faithfulness to all generations" (Psalm 100:4–5). This is clearly a song for corporate worship, a processional anthem for the road up to the temple. It refers to the gates of Jerusalem and the courts of the temple complex. But there may be another meaning as well. Giving thanks brings us into the Lord's presence. The gates may be these ideas of entitlement—as long as we think we deserve our blessings, there's a barrier between us and God. But we break through that gate when we humbly thank him for his grace.

A SONG SUNG TRUE

"I will sing of the mercies of the Lord for ever: with my mouth will I make known thy faithfulness to all generations" (Psalm 89:1 KJV). Apparently, a third way to respond to the Lord's mercies is to **sing** about them.

We have already seen how the apostle Paul wrote to the Philippians about joy, even though he was in prison. His inconvenient confinement was just an "adventure wrongly considered," you might say. Paul must have had a great deal of credibility with the Philippians because of what happened during his first trip to Philippi. He and his associate Silas were thrown in jail for casting a demon out of a fortune-teller (which was bad for the fortune-telling business). What did they do in their deep, dank prison? "About midnight Paul and Silas were praying and singing hymns to God, and the prisoners were listening to them" (Acts 16:25).

They sang! Not only did they see the blessings of God in a seemingly God-forsaken place, they were also thankful, and their gratitude erupted into song—which then affected the others around them. They were "making known" God's faithfulness "to all generations"—not just the other prisoners but also the members of the Philippian church, who would hear about it later, and 21st-century believers like us who are inspired by this moment.

How will you sing the daily blessings of God? And how will those around you be affected by your song?

A moment ago, we looked at the temple courts in Jerusalem. Psalm 136 was often sung in that setting. "O give thanks to the Lord, for he is good," the Levite musicians would intone, and the congregation would sing back, "for his steadfast love endures forever."

"O give thanks to the God of gods!"

"For his steadfast love endures forever."

The call-and-response would continue for 26 verses, with the song leaders detailing the Lord's actions throughout history.

"[God] spread out the earth on the waters...."
"For his steadfast love endures forever."
"...and divided the Red Sea in two...."
"For his steadfast love endures forever."
"...and rescued us from our foes...."
"For his steadfast love endures forever."

This interactive psalm recognized that the Lord's steadfast love took shape in specific ways at specific times. The people of Israel benefited from his loving actions and wanted to give their thanks.

Wouldn't that be a great thing for your family to do? Could you list some of the things God has done for you? This list could include the big things—your home, job, success at school, or healings—but it could also include the many tiny mercies you've begun to recognize in your daily lives. Then sing or read your way through the list, with the whole family joining in a psalmlike refrain.

"God gave us this great home to live in...."
"For his steadfast love endures forever."
"...and helped Julie pass her math test...."
"For his steadfast love endures forever."
"...and brought the crocuses to full bloom...."
"For his steadfast love endures forever."
"...and gives us new mercies every morning...."
"For his steadfast love endures forever."

A Prayer from the Promise

*Open my eyes, Lord, to the great things
you do for me each day. Let me see your
blessings as I walk through this world.*

*Open my ears, Lord, to hear the tiny
hallelujahs in every bird's song, in every
store clerk's comment, in every musical riff.*

*Open my heart, Lord, to be utterly
surprised and amazed by the intricate
ways you show your love for me.*

*I thank you, Lord, for your enduring love.
Amen.*

CHAPTER 5
You Will Have Troubles, But . . .

In this world you will have trouble.
But take heart!
I have overcome the world.

JOHN 16:33 NIV

His father was an editor, his mother an English teacher. You might say James had words in his blood. He had been writing since childhood—stories, plays, and articles. Teachers praised his creativity. A church group put on a Christmas drama he wrote. As a high school senior, James even got an article published in a national magazine. So, when he got to college, he eagerly registered for a creative writing course.

His professor, Dr. Daly, adored his work, from poems, to short stories, to journal entries. Whatever James put down on paper earned good grades and high praise. While other students would get their papers back with the corrective marks of Professor Daly's red pen, James would see only a bright red "A" and maybe a comment like

"Splendid! Just splendid!" It was great for his ego, and it didn't hurt his grade point average either.

The next semester, James signed up for a journalism course with Dr. Farmer, who had spent much of her adult life working for newspapers and magazines. James expected to sail through with another easy A.

When he got his first assignment back, he was shocked to find red marks all over it. "This makes no sense," read one comment. "Support this!" said another. Yet another demanded "More details!" James worked hard on the second piece he wrote for class but just got more red scribbles. In the first month of class, none of James's assignments earned higher than a B-minus. James researched like never before. He checked, double-checked, and triple-checked facts. Previously, it had seemed as if his writing spilled onto the page straight from his brain, but now he worked through multiple revisions before handing anything in.

"I don't know how much more of this I can take," he wrote to his best friend back home. "This is more work than any of my other classes, and I'll still be lucky to pull a B. Farmer knows her stuff, I guess, but she's not giving me any breaks. This is very discouraging. I used to think I could write."

James thought about dropping the course, but he stuck with it. Eventually, he earned a B for the semester and was delighted to get it. During the following summer, his father asked who his best teacher had been so far at college.

"Oh, I bet it was that writing prof," his mom suggested. "Dr. Daly? He loved your work so much."

"No," James answered. "Now that I think about it, Daly didn't teach me very much. He was a nice guy—and good for my confidence—but I learned so much more from Dr. Farmer. It was the hardest course I've ever had, but I really think it made me a better writer."

You might have a similar story in your own history. There are teachers, bosses, and coaches who make us feel better about ourselves, and that's important sometimes, but then there are others who actually make us better at what we do. The hardest teachers are often the best. The most challenging lessons often change us the most.

Of course, we might say the same thing about all of our life experiences. It feels good to have times of ease, when things go well. When your career, your relationships, and your creative endeavors all go well, you feel great. It's like being in school and getting a bright red A on every paper you turn in.

The hardest teachers are often the best.
The most challenging lessons
often change us the most.

But what happens when things stop going your way? You get laid off, there's tension in your marriage, or you have health issues. You make some bad decisions and you feel unappreciated and unimportant. Your self-confidence takes a nosedive because you just can't seem to get anything higher than a B-minus in your life.

Yet, these are the times that you grow the most. These struggles make you a better person.

TROUBLE BREWING

In his gospel, John spends several chapters recording the conversation Jesus had with his disciples at the Last Supper. It was a Passover meal that they enjoyed together at a home in Jerusalem, but there was tension in the air.

Jesus had been a public figure for about three years, but most of his activity had been in Galilee, well north of Israel's capital city. With his critical comments and populist preaching, Jesus had already roused the opposition of religious leaders. Now he had brought his ministry right to their doorstep. During the holiday, Jerusalem teemed with energy as crowds of pilgrims visited the temple. Jesus could preach in public and then disappear into the celebrating throng. All week he dodged his enemies, but then they enlisted one of his own disciples to betray him, and Jesus knew it. Things were about to get very difficult for him and for his followers. In what amounted to a farewell address, he prepared them for life after he was gone.

"In this world you will have trouble," he said. "But take heart! I have overcome the world" (John 16:33 NIV). In earlier versions of this passage the Greek word used for trouble, *thlipsis,* literally means "pressure." Life will come pressing down on you, Jesus says. At the time, he was addressing the physical threat of arrest, torture, or death that faced his followers. Within a few hours, a band of soldiers invaded their prayer garden to arrest Jesus. There was a skirmish involving Peter, but in the darkness, the disciples got away. Over the following days they met in secret, afraid to go public as followers of the crucified Galilean. They definitely felt pressure.

Their troubles were to be expected,
but they knew there would ultimately be victory,
as Jesus had overcome the world.

Over the next few years following Jesus' resurrection and ascension, Peter and John were arrested, beaten, and warned not to preach about Jesus. Then, the same tribunal that convicted Jesus tried the deacon Stephen, and he was stoned to death. John's brother, James, was killed by royal order. The followers of Christ certainly experienced the pressures of persecution.

This persecution intensified throughout the next three centuries. Emperor Nero blamed Christians for a disastrous fire in Rome and launched a bloody campaign of retaliation. Crosses bearing executed Christians lined the Appian Way. Later, other emperors picked up where Nero left off, sending Christians to face gladiators or wild beasts in the arena.

We can only guess how often these persecuted believers comforted one another with Jesus' words. Their troubles were to be expected, but they knew there would ultimately be victory, as Jesus had overcome the world.

One of the most amazing phenomena in history is that the Christian church actually grew in the face of fierce persecution from the Roman Empire. One important factor is that people saw the courage of Christians in the gladiatorial arena as they faced brutal death with unrelenting faith. As one Christian leader said, "The blood of the martyrs is the seed of the church." Christianity remained a force to be reckoned with, and eventually, the persecutors gave up. In the early fourth century A.D., after two-and-a-half centuries of opposition, Christianity was legalized and then adopted as the official religion of the empire. As some scholars have pointed out, there was a 250-year war between the greatest empire on Earth and the Christians, but only one side was fighting. We can see who was victorious.

Sadly, the persecution of Christians has occurred at various times since then. For much of the last century, China was the site of official persecution of Christians. As in the early church, believers had to meet in secret. But policies have eased in recent years, and we suddenly see a thriving Chinese church coming out from underground, with millions of devout believers made stronger by their difficulties.

Sometimes American Christians complain of being "persecuted" for their faith, but to be honest, we have it pretty easy. There may be discrimination in some corners of society, and we might face personal antagonism from some people we know, but there's nothing that compares with second-century Rome or twentieth-century China. In the New Testament, Peter wrote some interesting things on that subject. "Always be ready to make your defense to anyone who demands from you an account of the hope that is in you; yet do it with gentleness and reverence. Keep your conscience clear, so that, when you are maligned, those who abuse you for your good conduct in Christ may be put to shame. For it is better to suffer for doing good, if suffering should be God's will, than to suffer for doing evil" (1 Peter 3:15–17).

Note that our interaction with nonbelievers (even persecutors) should be characterized by "gentleness and reverence." If we do need to suffer, we should suffer because of our faith and not because we've been obnoxious. This raises the question that might come out of John 16:33—*how* does Jesus overcome the world? The Book of Revelation depicts Jesus in the end times as a conquering hero, but in the meantime he works through his followers, not in violence but in love.

For it is better to suffer doing good,
if suffering should be God's will,
than to suffer for doing evil.

1 PETER 3:15–17

TRIAL SIGHS

At the Last Supper, Jesus may have been talking about the persecution his disciples would face, but he might also have been speaking more generally. The truth is, we face pressure in our lives from many sources. Troubles and trials abound, and not just because we're believers, but because we're human. The New Testament portrays the whole universe "groaning" along with us as we await our ultimate redemption (Romans 8:22–23). Someday the Lord will set all things right, but for now we suffer the trials of ill health, broken relationships, destructive habits, and bad breaks.

But Paul also tells us, "I consider that the sufferings of this present time are not worth comparing with the glory about to be revealed in us" (Romans 8:18). To what is he referring? Our future redemption, when God turns everything around. Our heavenly bliss, as he wipes the tears from our eyes. His coming kingdom, where he crowns us to rule along with him. What a glorious day that will be!

Yet the kingdom always seems to have a double quality to it. It is in the future but also in the present. Aspects of the kingdom of glory tiptoe into our earthly lives and surprise us. Say you have a loved one confined to bed with an illness, but suddenly that person exudes spiritual wisdom. While the illness is indeed troubling, it's as if everything else in the person's life is now in order and God's glory comes beaming through. Or maybe you've seen someone display glorious courage in the aftermath of a tragic accident. Perhaps you have personally explored new corners of compassion in caring for a broken friend. In the midst of our trials, God's glory is revealed in us—not only in the future but right now, in some surprising ways.

RECEIVING THE PROMISE

So what are we to do with Jesus' promise? At the most basic level, it's both good news and bad news. It means we will have a life of struggle, but that we will ultimately overcome it. How can you handle that?

First, **remember that troubles are not unusual.** Some folks worry that God is punishing them for some sin and that he presents us with trials to get back at us. While it's true that our troubles are the product of a broken, sinful world, God is certainly not singling you out. Jesus' statement makes it clear that we should all expect hard times as part of our earthly life.

Then, **take comfort in the overcoming.** Jesus has already won the war. His crucifixion dealt a deathblow to the forces of destruction, and his resurrection was the final punch. Throughout history, some bloody battles have been fought *after* wars were officially over. Treaties were signed, but the armies didn't know yet. That's sort of what we're dealing with. We struggle against forces of brokenness that don't yet know they've lost.

Finally, **look for the glory.** Sure, you could spend some quality time musing about the heavenly elation ahead of you, but also look at your current situation. See how you are growing through a crisis. Aren't you stronger in character than you were before? And think of the deepening of your relationship with the Lord, who has also suffered. These positive aspects won't erase your pain, but they will help you through your troubles. You will find God's glory in your trials, if you look for it.

A Prayer from the Promise

Nobody knows the trouble I've seen—except you, Lord. Sometimes I feel torn, broken, wounded, and empty. I've been struggling to get through each day, trying to find strength in my faith, but sometimes people mock me for doing that. It's not easy.

You tell me this is normal and that I should expect to face pressures, trials, troubles, and persecution in my life. Thank you for that reassurance. Seriously, it does help a little to know that I don't have some rare case of divine displeasure.

But you have overcome the world. I'm sure that means a lot more than I can grasp right now, but I'm going to grab hold of that idea and cling to it. You have overcome! Keep showing me all the angles of that truth. What does that mean in my daily life? How can I taste some of that glory?

I will keep clinging to you, trusting you, learning from you, and counting on you to get me through. Thank you for helping me. In your loving power, Amen.

CHAPTER 6
I Will Strengthen You

✦❈✦

Do not be afraid,
for I am your God;
I will strengthen you,
I will help you.

ISAIAH 41:10

Chad's first job out of college was assistant to an associate in the marketing department of a sizable company. After a few months on the job, he was sent on a business trip across the country to interview distributors and hold some customer roundtables. The trip was originally scheduled for his boss, Sheila, but she had a minor family crisis, so Chad was left to nervously make his first foray out of the office.

A few days into the trip, Chad called Sheila to report on his progress. He had just returned to his motel room after a long day of meetings.

"What's that I hear in the background?" Sheila asked. "Are people shouting at you? Where are you?"

"I'm in my motel. It's the people in the next room. They argue all the time. Honestly, I've had trouble sleeping. This place is a real dive."

"Did you say *motel?* You're not at one of the big hotels downtown?"

"Oh, I couldn't afford that," Chad replied. "Not that I'm complaining about my pay. I just have lots of student loans to pay off, so I need to pinch pennies."

There was a brief silence on the line. "The company pays for your business expenses, you know."

"Really?"

"Sure," Sheila continued. "You turn in your receipts and they reimburse you for your hotels, rental cars, and meals. They plan on a $200 or $300 per diem for trips like this."

"Meals?" Chad asked. "They'll pay for my meals too? I've been eating fast food every day."

"Absolutely," Sheila laughed. "You can go to any restaurant you like. Just save your receipts."

"So all of that is covered?"

"Sorry, Chad. I thought you knew."

That little parable expresses a sad truth about many believers nowadays. We go through our lives scrimping on spiritual power; we "pinch pennies," so to speak. God has inestimable resources available to us and has promised to give us strength, help, and comfort—if we only request it.

This book has examined some of those divine promises, and you can find many more in the pages of Scripture. We have seen that God will be there when we seek him, that he loves and forgives us, and that our lives will have both trials and blessings. In this last chapter we'll zero in on a few practical commitments God makes to empower us.

God has inestimable resources available to us and has promised to give us strength, help, and comfort—if we only request it.

HELP WHEN YOU'RE TEMPTED

Have you ever wondered about this line in the Lord's Prayer: "Lead us not into temptation"? What's that about? Why would God ever lead us *into* temptation? Why would we have to ask him not to do that?

The situation gets even more perplexing when we compare a few other Bible passages. James tells us we should never say, "I am being tempted by God," for God himself "tempts no one" (James 1:13). And yet Matthew 4:1 informs us that "Jesus was led up by the Spirit into the wilderness to be tempted by the devil." That is, the Spirit of God did to Jesus exactly what we ask God not to do to us. What gives?

Some Bible teachers make a strong distinction between *tempting* and *testing*. While God may test our faith, they say, he will not tempt us to commit sin. That is a good way of looking at things, but it still doesn't answer everything. James tells us to rejoice when we face temptations, because it proves our faith and develops our endurance. We might say that every temptation tests our faith. If we resist, it's a helpful test. If we do not, it's a harmful temptation.

But elsewhere we find a valuable promise. Writing to the Corinthians, Paul said, "No testing [temptation] has overtaken you that is not common to everyone. God is faithful, and he will not let you be tested beyond your strength, but with the testing he will also provide the way out so that you may be able to endure it" (1 Corinthians 10:13).

The church of Corinth was situated in a spiritual battle zone. Corinth was a seaport that was filled with vice. The worship of idols—from traditional Greek gods to deities introduced by travelers from the east—was common. The Christian population struggled with specific issues of sexual immorality, church practice, and how to interact with their idol-worshipping neighbors. Aren't you glad we don't have those kinds of problems today?

Actually, we do. Only the "idols" of our culture tend to be things like money, celebrities, and sports. We are frequently tempted, not only by lust, but also by greed, pride, covetousness, and sloth. These temptations are all around us and they're so prevalent that it's almost impossible to resist. When we turn on the TV, we're tempted. When we log on to the Internet, temptation is there. When we go out for a drive, billboards lure us in one direction or another. We can't get away from temptation! Should we just give in now and ask forgiveness later?

———⌣———

God is faithful,
and he will not let you be tested
beyond your strength,
but with the testing
he will also provide the way out
so that you may be able to endure it.
1 CORINTHIANS 10:13

———⌣———

No, says Paul. As bad as temptation is, it has been around since the Garden of Eden. As dominant as it seems, there is an even stronger power available to us. God can be trusted to ensure that temptation does not overpower us. Presumably he can do this by shielding us from temptation (making it weaker), by building our righteous resolve (making us stronger), or providing a way out—in essence delivering us from evil.

So when we pray, "Lead us not into temptation, but deliver us from evil," we are acknowledging that dealing with temptation is difficult and we'd rather not go through it. But if God insists on leading us to a place where our faith will be tested, we need to ask him to lead us straight *through* it and deliver us from succumbing to temptation.

What tempts you? Is there an action you shouldn't do or an attitude you shouldn't have? Is there a harmful relationship you cling to or a good relationship you harm? You know how strong temptation is, but God is greater. You don't have to give in to temptation. God promises you the strength to fight temptation and, when you can't fight anymore, he provides a way out. That's a promise worth clinging to.

OUR AWESOME GOD

✻ ✻ ✻

Our God is an awesome God....

Perhaps you have sung those words in a worship service. Or maybe you've sung, "How Great Thou Art." In any case, you've learned that the power of God is truly awesome. We can see his great handiwork in nature and marvel at how great the Creator of such marvels must be. But occasionally there is a disconnection as we try to access that power in our own lives.

If your TV screen suddenly goes dark, you don't lose faith in the power company. Assuming that your lights are still on, you believe that the power lines still course with all the electricity you need and there's just a problem with your set. Something has stopped the power from getting to the TV.

Many believers have a similar problem in their spiritual lives. They truly trust in the awesome power of God but find it hard to get that power into their lives. There's a short circuit, a blown fuse, or a bad wire somewhere.

We struggle with temptation. We doubt whether we have the ability to do anything important for God. We feel distracted by our daily responsibilities. We carry the guilt of past sin. Any of these issues can disconnect us from God's power supply.

"I will strengthen you," the Lord tells us. "I will help you, I will uphold you with my victorious right hand.... For I, the Lord your God, hold your right hand; it is I who say to you, 'Do not fear, I will help you'" (Isaiah 41:10, 13).

First, we see God's right hand. In ancient Hebrew thinking, the right hand was a symbol of strength, as it was the warrior's best weapon. The Lord's right hand, or his strength, gains victory after victory. But do you see the next picture in this biblical slide show? That awesome, all-victorious right hand of God holds *our* hand. If you try to visualize this, the image is not like two lovers strolling the beach hand-in-hand. That would be nice, but here *his right hand* holds *our right hand.* Visualize instead a parent teaching a child how to swing a baseball bat, shoot a free throw, or fly a kite. The parent guides the child with their right hand on their child's right hand. In the same way, God's strength and skill is transmitted to our weak, unskilled hands. He works through us.

Very truly, I tell you,
the one who believes in me will also
do the works that I do and, in fact,
will do greater works than these....
If in my name you ask me for anything,
I will do it.

JOHN 14:12, 14

Perhaps the most amazing divine promise in Scripture touches on this very point. In his conversation with his disciples at the Last Supper, Jesus said, "Very truly, I tell you, the one who believes in me will also do the works that I do and, in fact, will do greater works than these.... If in my name you ask me for anything, I will do it" (John 14:12, 14).

The disciples included fishermen, a tax collector, a frustrated revolutionary, and a handful of other guys we still know very little about. And they were to do greater works than Jesus? Yeah, right. After all, Jesus had dazzled a nation for three years, healing the blind and lame, stilling storms, and raising the dead. How could these average Joes do any better than that? A few hours after Jesus told them this, the disciples had to run for their lives, since they lacked the courage to stand up for their leader. How could they possibly do anything *great,* much less *greater* than Jesus?

Note that the promise extends beyond the disciples to anyone "who believes in me." That's us, right? But how could we possibly do things any greater than Jesus did? Only with God's hand on our hand, with his promises in our heads, and with his name in our hearts.

A Prayer from the Promise

What am I supposed to do with this, Lord?
Do you really expect me to do greater
things than Jesus did? I don't doubt your
power. I'm just not sure I have
the right connection.

The fact is, I deal with a zillion temptations
in my life, and not always successfully.
I am truly sorry for my sin, and I'll try to
do better, but that's the problem.
I lack the moral strength to resist
temptation. So, if you mean business about
showing me a way out, I'll take you up
on that. Lead me not into temptation, but
deliver me from evil. I definitely need your
strength to do that, because my strength
alone isn't enough.

And if you really want me to do powerful
things in this world, I will, but I can only
do them with your power.

Work through me. In your name,
Amen.